CAMPCRAFT FIELD COOKBOOK

CAMPCRAFT FIELD COOKBOOK

EASY RECIPES FOR CAMP, CABIN, AND ALONG THE TRAIL

Jason A. Hunt

JAMIE BURLEIGH & GREG LAUGHLIN

Barefoot Prophet Media

Contents

Contents

vii

Acknowledgments

I would like to recognize the Campcraft Outdoor instructors, specifically Mike Sommesi, Jamie Burleigh, Greg Laughlin, John Dosch, and Ethan Hoell, who all have played a critical part in developing the *Fat Camp*, as we affectionately refer to our school. Your recipes, some of which are shared here, have fueled many hungry souls. Thank you for your ongoing friendship, for teaching me as much as I have taught you, and for sharing all the meals and the laughs. If you were not here for all the recipes in this book, you were certainly thought of while they were made.

Special thanks to the many students I have met and trained with. Thank you for participating in our food creation labs around the campfire.

Most of all, thank you to my wife, Robyn. Despite cooking for so many people over the years and now writing a cookbook, she still doesn't make me cook at home on the regular. For that, I am grateful.

Introduction

I'm thankful to be able to present our initial *Campcraft Field Cookbook* with contributions from my long-time friends and instructors, Jamie Burleigh and Greg Laughlin. We are not trained chefs, but we all like to eat. As the saying goes, *always trust a fat survivalist.* Our kitchen training is limited to casual dining restaurants we worked in as young men and a big bag of tricks we picked up over the years from people with good ideas. Experience has been our greatest teacher. We all love to serve people; it's part of our faith in Jesus Christ, which carries over to an innate desire to see people enjoying the hard times we put them through while training in outdoor skills. We have learned there is no greater place to relate to people than over a campfire meal. We have seen people's lives change through the process of preparing, cooking, and eating together. That may sound like a radical notion, but we have seen people on the brink of self-harm, broken marriages, battling depression, and just having a plain old bad week reform their outlook, and change their minds and hearts within an hour or two through some Godly fellowship preparing a meal. It's such a common theme at our school we just accept the naturally supernatural things that occur every time we have a group of people here. There's a gospel ministry hidden in feeding people, and many fail to see it.

To partner together to write this cookbook is a great blessing for us. There is much more we could include and other instructors that could add so much more to this project; we hope that an expanded edition will permit us to one day build upon the foundation we lay here.

Regarding measurements used in this text, we rarely use exact measurements in camp. We do everything by eye and to taste, but we use the old-time hand measurements, which we'll share in detail, and the same cooking gear every time, which enables us to get fairly accurate measurements for everything. When necessary, we provided measurements in the following manner:

- T = Tablespoon
- tsp. = Teaspoon
- c. = Cup, 8oz
- lb. = pound

You can easily adjust as you desire from these amounts within each recipe. I also strive to maintain a clean cooking environment, and I am big on hygiene, especially when cooking for other people. I clean my cook space often and do not cross-contaminate; while this takes additional time and effort in the field, it's worth it. I do not want my cooking to be why someone has a bad outdoor trip. Please, take the time to clean, sanitize, and wipe down your tools, prep, and cook area often.

The recipes in this book will boost morale and mend life's problems for many hungry souls wherever time is spent training outdoors. We sincerely hope you will seize every opportunity to share your faith, listen to a friend vent, and counsel a lost traveler along the trail as you cook. Many of our friendships have been forged around these meals that continue today. Some of our most emboldened recipes came around trappers' camps where it was unknown whether or not certain critters would make adequate table fare. Thankfully, these camps provided the lab for experimentation, always met with the resounding approval of seasoned woodsmen and those well versed in camp cookery. Now, after logging thousands of miles and leading thousands of students along trails across a quarter of the United States, we'd like to share a sampling of what we do at "*Fat Camp*," Campcraft Outdoors, through this Field Cookbook.

We hope to share a campfire tale and meal with you in the future,
Jason Hunt

1

Old Woods Cook Hacks

The wisdom of older generations can be found in the lore told around the campfire. Tips and tricks used for generations we now call hacks that make life easier or better. These camp cooking hacks will enable you to tap into the wisdom of a bygone era while improving your camp life.

1. Cooking in Iron Pots.—Let nothing stand in an iron pot after it is cooked, or it will become discolored and have an unpleasant taste.
2. Rusty Knives.—If knives become rusty, rub them with a fresh-cut potato dipped in ashes.
3. Save the Bacon Grease.—Do not discard the grease left in the pan after frying salt pork, bacon, or fat meat. Keep a cup or small tin pail, in which pour all residue. It will soon harden and is just the thing for frying slapjacks or potatoes in.
4. Improved River Water for Drinking.—If you make tea, do not throw out the "grounds" after each drawing. In warm weather, ordinary lake or river water will taste very refreshing if poured into the pot where tea grounds have been left and allowed to stand a few minutes before drinking.

5. Salt.—It is always best in cooking to use too little salt rather than too much. Further salting can be easily done at any time, but it is difficult or impossible to freshen anything that has been over-salted.

6. Baking Powder.—In using baking powder, it is always best to follow the printed directions on the can as to the amount. The different makes of baking powders have different strengths.

7. Spoons.—On a canoe trip, where storage room is at a premium, one spoon will suffice for all purposes. Let it be of iron, of "dessert" size. Get a tinsmith to cut off two inches of the handle and solder strongly to the stump a tin cylinder one-half inch in diameter. There will be no long handle to interfere with packing it in a small space, and if a long handle is desired for skimming soups, stirring mush, etc., a stick of any length can be instantly cut to fit the tin cylinder.

8. Frozen Fish should be soaked in cold water to thaw them before cooking.

9. Fish-eating Ducks may be palatable by parboiling them in water with an onion. After parboiling them throw away the onion and lay the ducks in cold water for half an hour, after which they may be roasted, broiled, fried, or stewed.

10. Soft vs. Hard Water.—Beans, peas, and other vegetables are best boiled in soft water. Hard water can be turned soft by boiling it for an hour and then allowing it to cool when most of the lime will be precipitated.

11. Broiling.—Remember that it is better to broil before a fire than over it, as by the former process, the juices of the meat can be caught and used as a dressing, while in the latter manner, they are lost in the fire and tend to give a smoky flavor by their ignition. In broiling, the food should be turned frequently.

12. Frying.—The lard or fat used for frying should always be very hot before the article to be cooked is put in. If little jets of smoke issue from the top of the fat, it is hot enough. If the fat is

insufficiently hot, anything cooked in it will taste of the grease, while the moment a substance is dropped into fat at a great heat, the exterior pores are closed, and no grease penetrates it.

13. New Iron Pots.—Boil a handful of grass in a new iron pot, scrub it inside with soap and sand, fill it with clean water, and let it boil for half an hour. It is then ready to use for cooking.

2

Measurements without Utensils

Woodsmen have long measured ingredients without the need for proper utensils. Once you get the hang of these substitutions and equivalents, they will eliminate a lot of the worry about exacting recipe measurements.

Hand Measurements

- 1 Open Fistful = 1/2 cup
- Five-Finger Pinch = 1 Tablespoon
- Four-Finger Pinch = 1 Teaspoon
- One-Finger Pinch(with thumb) = 1/8 Teaspoon
- One-Finger Gob of shortening = 1 Tablespoon
- Palm of hand (center) = 1 Tablespoon

Fluid Standard Measures

- 3 Teaspoons = 1 Tablespoon = 1/2 oz = 29.57 milliliters
- 16 Tablespoons = 1 Cup = 8 oz = 0.236 liters

- 2 Cups = 1 Pint = 16 oz = 0.473 liters
- 2 Pints = 1 Quart = 32 oz = 0.946 liters
- 4 Quarts = 1 Gallon = 128 oz = 3.785 liters
- 1 Gallon = 8 lbs.

Substitutions and Equivalents

- 1 lb. butter / shortening = 2 cup
- 4 oz. cheddar cheese = 1 cup grated
- 1/2 pt. whipping cream = 1 cup (2 c. whipped)
- 8 oz. sour cream = 1 cup = 1 cup plain low-fat yogurt
- 1 lb. flour = app. 3 1/2 cup
- 1 cup marshmallows = 11 large or 110 miniature
- 1 lb. brown sugar = 2 1/4 cup (packed)
- 1 lb. granulated sugar = 2 1/4 cup
- 1 cup milk = 1/2 cup evaporated milk + 1/2 cup water = 1 cup reconstituted dry milk + 2 tbs. butter
- 1 cup buttermilk = 1 cup milk + 1 tbs. vinegar
- 1 cup sour milk = 1 cup sweet milk + 1 Tbs. vinegar/ lemon juice
- 1 stick buffer = 1/4 lb. or 1/2 cup or 8 tbs.
- 1 lb. loaf bread = about 17 slices
- 1 cup of fine crumbs = 22 vanilla wafers, 4 slices of bread, 26 saltine
- crackers,14 graham crackers
- 1 Tbs. instant minced onion = 1 small fresh onion
- 1 Tbs. prepared mustard = 1 tsp. dry mustard
- 1 cup sugar = 2/3 to 3/4 cup honey
- 1 cup honey = 1 cup molasses
- 1 whole egg = 2 egg whites = 1/4 cup egg substitute= 1 egg white + 1 tsp. oil
- 1 oz baking chocolate = 3 Tbs. cocoa powder + 1 Tbs. oil

- 1 Tbs. cornstarch (for thickening) = 2 Tbs. flour

3

Solo Cook Kits

I have found it most convenient to pack light when camping over a weekend. I do not go into the woods to eat but to unplug from work and the stresses of life to commune with God through creation. I like to take a *Campcraft Pantry* for my snacks and one main meal that can be prepared in the nested cup of my water bottle. The Campcraft Pantry is based on a 1940s food vault used by the Scouts. It comprises six 16oz stainless steel tins within a waxed canvas bag. This enables the user to have a waterproof, portable pantry in a single place within their pack. As the weather gets cooler, we like to eat more to stay warm, and this pantry does a nice job at providing the extra calories we need to maintain homeostasis.

Campcraft Pantry Food Sampling
Photo by Rocky Hollow

We usually carry Jerky, Dried Fruit, Mixed Nuts, Rice, Oats, and a Soup Mix in the tins. The rice, oats, and soup can easily be cooked in my nesting cup. Along with the pantry, I will bring a piece of meat, such as a steak that has been marinated and sealed in a food saver bag, a cottage ham, or an additional homemade meal-ready-to-eat (MRE). The homemade MRE offers an endless supply of possibilities. If you have a food saver or purchase freezer bags with a vacuum valve, you can create long-lasting MREs at home. A homemade MRE will cost you around three to five dollars, whereas a Military MRE will cost twelve or more. Here's the great news, if you plan to eat your MRE within a week of making it, you can feel confident in carrying precooked bacon with you. I will often include a Ramen package, strips of precooked bacon, some drink mixes, a granola bar, and mashed potatoes in mine. It expands my menu options and is very lightweight, and again, it can be cooked in my nesting cup without needing a skillet or larger pot.

**Kentucky Whiskey Ramen made with a homemade
MRE**

Foraged foods such as leeks, ramps, and onions can make a dull dish even better, and I include them whenever they are in season. Eggs, when desired, are best carried as hard-boiled, dehydrated, or freeze-dried. I have a home freeze dryer, so I can create various egg styles that transport well. Use your imagination and push yourself to experiment beyond your normal routine. You may stumble upon something amazing to your palate, as I have so many times.

Cooking Tools

Regarding the cook kit itself, I have two versions of it that I primarily use and recommend. I find that I carry a water filter with me most of the time I venture outdoors. Honestly, I've grown tired of boiling water to drink, having done it thousands of times over the last twenty years. I like the convenience of the Grayl Geopress and that it nests in all my camp mugs. When I carry my Grayl, I will most often carry a titanium cook stove that stows in my cook kit. I keep my Grayl in my day bag and my cook kit on my hip when I'm not hiking around more than a few miles.

Solo Cooking Kit: Nested Together

Solo Cooking Kit: Exploded View

I enjoy this titanium cooking kit. It's a Bestargot kit; the main pot had a bail and handle with a lid. It's a 750ml cup and fits on all my stainless steel water bottles and Grayl Geopress filter. The pot has an insulated koozie that allows the user to easily handle hot liquids. The smaller container is my bowl, made by the same company, and it nests under the main pot while in the koozie. The stove fuel and titanium stove drop into the pot when not in use, and I can store it all in the canvas bag seen in the background. I can carry it on my belt or toss it in my backpack. I'll carry the stove whenever I'm going into an area that prefers I do not use open fires.

Whenever I'm free to make a fire or when we're engaged in a training class, I'll never use a fuel stove. I'll instead carry a stainless steel water bottle which gives me another piece of kit that can be cooked in and can be used to boil additional water. I carry this kit on a shoulder sling bag and sometimes stow it in my backpack, but rarely. I carry a shoulder-slung kit when I plan to travel throughout the day, so I always have ready access to my water bottle.

Shoulder-slung Cook Kit with Steel Bottle

This simple cooking kit system will keep you well fed and lighten your load with a little practice. Once you learn how to make things easier, it's hard to go back to complicate things with all the modern gadgets and gizmos that come out yearly with the latest technological advancements. If I need to charge, replace regularly, or upkeep my core cooking items beyond a simple cleaning, they're probably not worth using.

Solo Cooking Kits

4

Group Cook Kits

Moving beyond a solo trip, we're going to look at what I recommend as a minimum cooking kit for a small group of four or five people. If camping with adults, it's common for everyone to bring their eating utensils and have a plan to cook. Regardless of their best-laid plans, I have always taken it upon myself to bring enough gear for everyone to eat or cook. I've lifted heavy weights in the gym to carry heavy loads in the woods! Well, that's the tale I tell my wife anyway. A small group cooking kit need not be burdensome, and thankfully owning a canvas manufacturing business has its perks- we have created ways to carry our gear more efficiently and have proven them to work through expeditions around the country.

Using 2QT Pots as Flat tops during a class

The 2-quart Bushpot is the foundation of the small group camp. You can get four healthy servings from a single pot. You can also bake in the pot when turned on its side and cook on the bottom as a flat-top griddle. Many a bannock cake has been made on the bottom of these pots. I prefer a stainless steel pot over the anodized or aluminum models, merely for heat distribution and durability. I add four stainless steel plates to this kit as well. I can fry or cook on these plates as needed, and they clean easily for serving once they cool. The plates nest under the bushpot. Inside the bushpot, I place my 750ml cup, the same one used in my solo cooking kit, but this one is steel. Inside the 750ml cup, I stow a small camp mug used for refreshments and as a measuring cup. I'll also include a military can opener in the pot, a clean bandanna, and my dry seasonings for the trip.

I carry a *Utensil Roll* that I hang above my food prep area. The roll holds my spatula, tongs, and eating utensils for the group and myself.

Utensil Roll hanging above my prep area

Please remember that none of my recommendations are meant to sway you. The kits explained and shown are what I have used for many years to create hundreds of meals; these have worked for me. Glean whatever you can from these recommendations and make your adjustments accordingly.

In the cooler months or when the group is planning a serious cook, I add a 1-gallon Bushpot or Stainless Steel Milk Bucket to my kit, along with an 8" folding skillet. This works well in cooking large meals during inclement weather and allows me to boil water and cook simultaneously to keep the hot drinks flowing without disrupting my cooking process. Again, all of this nests together, and I stow it away in one bag made for the purpose. I have been using the Pathfinder brand stainless steel cookware for years. When I worked as the Operations Manager at Pathfinder School, I was able to use and abuse the gear, and there's no fault in it. As far as milk buckets, you can easily get stainless steel buckets and bowls from most farm stores or online. They make for an affordable alternative to purpose-built bushpots.

Group Cooking Kits in their respective bags: 2QT on Left, Gallon on Right

My kits can be carried on my belt or in a backpack. I've shlepped these kits across a mile of open water swimming in the Gulf of Mexico to a key and dragged them across untold miles of Appalachian Jungle with thorns and briars so thick, grown men have cried (I have photos!). My point is that these kits, as they are, weigh little, considering all they are capable of. Choose a system you can manage to carry on foot for at least five miles at a time without undue stress on your body. This will make your trip and cooking experiences much more enjoyable.

Jason A. Hunt

What I keep in the 2-quart Bushpot Bag

The nested system within the Large Bushpot Bag

5

Base Camp Cook Kit

Breakfast cooking at camp on a raised cooking bed

Conveyance is the key to a good base camp kitchen. If you have a way to transport all your cooking gear, then the sky is the limit. Whenever access by vehicle or UTV is permitted near a campsite, I always go with my cast iron. To be honest, there have also been times when I spread out my heavy cooking gear among the students I was training and made them carry it all for me. But, generally speaking, cast iron should be reserved for a base camp operation where you have the ability to transport it rather than carrying it.

Besides cast iron, there are other tools we regularly use, such as discadas, fryers, propane cookers, camp stoves, and tripods. A discada is a cooking disc, like a shallow wok, made popular by migrant farmers. They used to be made from plow discs in the field where tortillas could be made and cooked along with nearly anything else. They are very convenient and are now mass-produced in lighter-weight materials for the average camper. What you use will depend on your group size and what you are comfortable using. More is not always better; it will take trial and error to figure out what sizes and how many skillets and pots you need to care for your standard groups. Having fed small groups and as large as 200 at one time; I can speak from experience that a single large skillet and a single dutch oven with a small group cook kit can feed twenty with ease if you stage your servings right and plan your menu accordingly.

In my base camp cook kit, it's pretty standard. If I have a larger group, I have two options: add another skillet or oven, or use a larger skillet or oven (I have a 5-gallon Dutch Oven!). Adding another is the least expensive option if you are just starting out.

My Standard Base Camp Kit is:

- 1: 12" Dutch Oven
- 1: Reflector Oven
- 1: Folding Grill (Optional)
- 1: Small Group Cook Kit
- 1: Cooking Gloves
- 1: Utensil Roll (Knife, Spatula, tongs, spoons, and forks)

This is the kit I use for the majority of my outdoor classes. I piggyback on my small group cook kit with an improved utensil roll and some cast iron cookware. The reflector oven is one of the most under-rated items a camp cook can use- I love mine, which was gifted to me by a wise friend and camp cook. They're expensive and worth every penny. However, you can make one from foil and cookie sheets that work nearly as well for a fraction of the cost.

I have my full base camp kitchen set up when it's time to show off or when I know we will be food-heavy due to it being cold or a longer camp. Remember that this is only the cooking kit, not accessory items helpful for washing, seasoning, or food specific.

Here is what my Large Group (20+ people) kit consists of:

- 1: 12" Dutch Oven
- 1: 16" Dutch Oven
- 1: 12" Cast Iron Skillet
- 1: 17" Cast Iron Skillet
- 1: 24" Folding Grill
- 1: Reflector Oven
- 1: Gallon Bucket or Bushpot
- 2: Plastic Scraping Tools
- 1: 12" x 24" cutting board
- 1: Chainmail Scrubber
- 1: Propane Cooker with Tank
- 1: Discada
- 1: Fry Basket with Fry Pot
- 1: Utensil Roll for Cooking Only
- 2: Cooking Gloves (Welder style or insulated)
- 1: Small Shovel (for pit digging or fire maintenance)
- 10: Cooking rags
- 4: Steel Enamel Plates for shuttling food around

I realize this is a lot, but it's only for a large group I use it all. If I have a base camp operation, however, I can pull what I need out on any given day, clean it and store it without fear of not having something. It may change daily. But this setup allows me to do every recipe in this book and so much more with relative ease. Notice that cooking irons and a tripod are missing from this list. If I want a tripod, which is rare for me, then I'll make it from locally available tree limbs and some cordage. If I need to poke around the fire, I'll use my shovel or a stick.

**Frying fish for a hungry group of
students in a survival class**

If you plan on serving others or frying things, heavy paper plates, plastic utensils, and paper towels are a must. Paper plates and towels do not store well in the woods for very long due to rodents, bugs, and moisture, but stored in a sealed locking tote; you can keep them in an outdoor shelter for a long time. I prefer rags for oiling and cleaning my cookware. I can boil my rags to clean them, then hang them to dry in the sun or over a low fire instead of creating additional trash.

Greg monitoring the fish fry after the first round

Sharing a good camp meal with others can turn the most inhospitable camping experience into a fond memory that will have people itching to go back. It's often said that food prepared over a campfire tastes better, and while there is truth in that statement, it's all about the relationships you build that make cooking enjoyable. Seeing smiling faces, sharing a laugh, or repentant tears flowing into a bowl of chili, I sense God at work when good meals are shared between people.

Breakfast at Camp

"The comforts of life's essentials -- food, fire, and friendships..."
Julia Child

An early morning camp breakfast is a great way to start the day. We generally prefer a longer-lasting breakfast, something that will power us through dinner with little more than a snack at midday, and our recipes reflect that. When we engage in the activities that wild spaces offer, bushcraft, hiking, hunting, fishing, and exploration, we need long-burning energy to seize every opportunity.

Before striking camp or leaving our base for the day ahead, pack up all essential leftovers for later meals and the day's snacks, so the local critters have less of a reason to invade your camp and stores.

6

Robyn's Eggs

After camping with so many people over the past twenty years, I have yet to eat any eggs in camp as good as my wife's. Robyn isn't much of a cook, but a few things she just gets right, and eggs are one of those things. Growing up, I thought a scrambled egg was just an egg that you stirred up while it cooked in a skillet. While this recipe is not one of the more grandiose I have seen, it's one more camper need to use- I found breakfast eggs abhorrent until she showed me a few simple tricks after we married. Now, whenever I make eggs at camp, I get rave reviews. So here's one of Robyn's most basic egg recipes.

Ingredients

- 12 Eggs
- 1/4 c. Milk
- Salt & Pepper
- 1 c. Shredded Cheese

Steps

Whisk your eggs in a dish, then add 1 cup of milk. Whisk until well beaten, then salt and pepper to taste before adding in cheese. Now, cook until done. Your eggs will be fluffy and light, with cheese throughout. If you cook on a hot griddle in bacon or sausage grease, you can crisp the cheese more and have crunchiness to the eggs; some call it *dirty eggs*.

7

Drop Biscuits

Three-step biscuits take only 3 ingredients to make, are delicious, and allow them to be made at nearly every camp outing you may be involved in. Anytime you can serve warm biscuits with homemade preserves or butter is a great day.

Ingredients

- 2 c. self-rising flour
- 1 c. lard or butter (softened)
- 2/3 c. buttermilk

Biscuit dough dropped onto a baking sheet

Steps

Fold in the softened lard or butter to the flour until it looks like cornmeal, then mix in the buttermilk until a dough is formed. Spoon piles and drop them onto a baking sheet for the reflector or conventional oven and cook at 350 until golden brown.

Golden brown biscuit goodness

<table><tr><td>8</td></tr></table>

Fried Biscuits

I am always shocked when people are unaware of fried biscuits. They're similar to beignets, both of which were staples growing up. We always had canned biscuits or could whip up a biscuit-like dough to fry for a donut. We would often roll them in powdered sugar, top them with cinnamon and sugar, serve them with apple butter when in season, and, when available, top them with chocolate for various treats.

canned biscuits fried for a breakfast treat

Ingredients

- Biscuits (canned or drop biscuit recipe)
- Frying Oil
- Powdered sugar or another way to add flavor

Steps

In a Dutch oven or deep skillet, preheat fryer oil to 375 degrees. Prepare biscuits, then lay them in the hot oil. They will float once they partially cook; flip them in the oil, so both sides are golden brown, then cook for an additional 20 seconds to form a crunch and ensure the dough cooks through. Remove from oil and allow to rest as they will still be cooking inside for a moment. Once cooled, top with whatever toppings you have available and serve.

9

Cathead Biscuits & Sawmill Gravy

Woodsmen require a hearty meal to perform for long hours hiking, sawing, and building in the wilderness. Logger camps throughout Appalachia in the old days made Biscuits and Gravy a staple within their diet. Cathead biscuits get their name from the Mississippi Delta region; the biscuits were prepared as big as a cat's head. Sawmill Gravy often included sausage or bacon within the mixture. Still, I have it on good authority from sawyers that grew up in the Smoky and Blue Ridge Mountains that many mills would include whatever meats would pass musters, such as groundhog, rabbit, and squirrel. Regardless, it's tasty when you're craving a Southern classic.

You can cook biscuits in a preheated 425-degree oven. You may use a Coleman oven, Reflector oven, #10 can, or a Large Bush-pot turned on its side. You will have to monitor the fire more closely, so heat is nearly constant, and rotate the biscuits a couple of times through the cooking cycle.

This recipe will make six (6) biscuits
Ingredients

- 1 ½ c. all-purpose flour*
- 1 ½ c. cake flour*

*You may substitute 3 c. of Martha White or White Lily flour to give the desired loft and texture.

- 1 T. baking powder
- ½ tsp. baking soda
- 8 T. unsalted butter (cut into ½" pads and softened)
- 4 T. vegetable shortening (Crisco), cut into ½" pieces
- 1 ¼ c. buttermilk

Steps

Grease a 9-inch pan, and whisk together flour, baking powder, baking soda, and salt in a large bowl. Scatter the butter and shortening pieces across the top of the flour mixture and hand mix into the flour until it resembles a coarse meal. Now, stir in buttermilk until combined. Using a large spoon, drop 6 heaping mounds of the dough onto the greased pan. Bake until golden brown, about 20-25 minutes. Cool the biscuits for 10-minutes before serving (the most challenging part!).

Sawmill Gravy (enough to cover 6 biscuits)
Ingredients

- 1lb breakfast sausage
- ½ c. flour
- 4 cups milk
- Salt and Pepper

Steps

Cook the sausage in a cast iron skillet; whisk flour into the sausage fat for 5 minutes, remove from heat and whisk in the milk a little at a time. Replace on medium heat and stir until gravy thickens; scrape any brown bits from the side of the skillet back into the mixture for flavor bursts. Mix the sausage around and stir- it's ready to serve—season with salt and pepper to taste.

10

Camp Grits

Grits are often considered a breakfast dish, but honestly, they can be changed into a hearty meal any time of the day, with some manipulation. Grits have been used for centuries when better food was not available. During the Great Depression, people got very creative and created a variety of dishes from grits, including bread. Here are a few recipes to try at your next campout.

Common Grits

Ingredients

1 c. Corn Grits (course ground corn meal)
1/2 Tsp Salt
3 c. Water

Steps

Bring water and salt to a boil. Add Corn Grits and reduce heat. Cook slowly for about 5 minutes, stirring occasionally. Remove from heat, cover, and let stand for a couple of minutes. This will make enough for four generous helpings.

Quick Grits

Ingredients

- 1/2 c Instant Grits
- 1 T Bacon Bits
- Molly McButter

Steps

Boil Water, add grits, add bacon bits, and hit with a dash of Molly McButter to taste.

Hearty Grits

Ingredients

- 1/2 c Instant Grits
- 2 slices of chopped bacon
- 1/4 small onion, diced
- salt and pepper
- 1 tsp. minced garlic
- 2 pads of butter

Boil water and make grits according to directions as you cook bacon. While bacon is cooking, toss in onions with the bacon until translucent. Once grits are ready, mix in minced garlic and pads of butter. Top grits with bacon and onions, salt and pepper to taste.

Corn Grit Bread

Ingredients

- 2 c. Cooked Grits (see Common Grits Recipe)

- 2 T Melted Butter
- 2 Eggs
- 2 Tsp Salt
- ½ c. Milk
- Cheese (optional)

Steps

Add milk, salt, butter, and eggs to warm grits and stir until mixed well. Pour into greased pan. Bake at around 375°F for 30 minutes or until a toothpick inserted into the middle pulls out clean with no streaks. You can add cheese to the recipe or top the loaf with cheese for added variety.

11

Mountain Man Breakfast

Mountain Man Breakfast in a #12 Lodge Dutch Oven

While the origin of this casserole-style dish is unknown, it combines all of your favorite breakfast items into one pot. It works perfectly in the Dutch oven and is excellent in the home casserole dish. It's also versatile for hungry campers- you can serve it straight from the pot or add it to a tortilla wrap for hearty breakfast burritos.

Ingredients

- Salt & Pepper
- Cooking Oil or Lard
- 1lb Russett Potatoes – diced small; the larger they are, the longer they will take to cook. You can also substitute bagged hash browns of your preference.
- 1lb Breakfast sausage – ground, crumbled for easier cooking.
- 1-2 onion(s) – diced.
- 12 eggs – beaten and seasoned with salt and pepper.
- 1 c. Cheddar cheese – grated. We do not recommend pre-grated or shredded cheeses. These often have an anti-caking coating that alters the dish's flavor.
- Green onions – chopped to taste

Optional

- Large flour tortillas – if you're serving this burrito-style.
- Sour cream
- Sliced Jalapeno

Steps

Coat the Dutch oven with a layer of oil and allow it to preheat as you dice the potatoes and onions. Add the potatoes and onions to the Dutch oven, add light salt and pepper to taste, and allow to cook half-way, or for about 15-minutes. While the taters are cooking, beat the eggs and season with salt and pepper to taste. After 15 minutes, add the breakfast sausage to the Dutch oven and allow it to cook in the potatoes and onions until browned, then add eggs over the entire dish. Stir well, and allow to cook for about 6-minutes before stirring again. Cook until eggs are firm throughout, then remove from bottom heat. Add grated cheese and chopped green onion. Add coals (or 12 briquettes) to the lid of the Dutch oven to act as a broiler to melt the cheese (roughly 10 minutes). Serve when the cheese is melted!

12

Feral Scotch Eggs

The feral Scotch egg is a British dish consisting of a shelled hard-boiled egg wrapped in breakfast sausage, covered in breadcrumbs, and deep-fried until crispy made with feral hog. It's a popular dish commonly served cold in Britain and is a fantastic trail meal that can be carried for hours along the trail without fear of immediate spoilage. I have brought a couple of these with me on long humps wrapped in foil and held in my haversack.

A feral hog taken on my property in Kentucky

Ingredients

- 8 hard-boiled eggs
- 2 eggs, beaten
- 2lb hog meat, gound up or breakfast sausage
- 1/2c. seasoned breadcrumbs
- Salt and pepper to taste
- Oil for frying

Dip the hard-boiled eggs into the beaten eggs. Wrap each egg in roughly 1/4lb of sausage, then dip into the beaten eggs again before rolling in bread crumbs. Deep fry at 375 degrees for 5-6 minutes or until sausage is fully cooked, then allow to cool at least 5-minutes before serving. You may wrap these in foil to carry as a trail lunch or late-day snack as needed.

Feral Scotch Eggs

13

The Camp Skillet

If you have a skillet for each member in your camp, you can cook everything in the same skillet for a hearty camp skillet breakfast. Serve with a biscuit or pancakes on the side, and get the camp coffee on because this recipe plan is a sure-fire winner.

Ingredients

- 4 slices of Bacon or 2 Sausage patties
- 1 potato, grated (Hash Brown style)
- 2 Eggs
- Vegetable Oil (Frying oil)
- Biscuits (canned or scratch) or Pancakes*

In a cook or frying pot, heat cooking oil for frying (if making biscuits)

Prepare a griddle or Dutch Oven lid with a shot of oil to cook pancakes.

In a skillet, prepare bacon or sausage; roughly half way through cooking, drop in a handful of grated potato (hash browns) and allow to fry in the meat grease. Remove meat from the skillet when done, and finish potatoes as you crack eggs into the skillet. Cook as desired. Once eggs and potatoes are done, add the meat back into the skillet and allow it to rest.

Your fryer oil should now be up to temperature; fry canned or scratch-made biscuits until golden brown (4 minutes), drain, then serve in the skillet.

*Refer to the biscuit and pancake recipes shared in earlier sections.

Camp Dinners

"When you're down on your luck and lost all your dreams, there's nothing like a campfire and a can of beans."
-- Tom Waits, "Lucky Days"

The following campfire dinner recipes will keep you and your guests looking forward to camping opportunities. We have been tremendously blessed by the fellowship that's taken place around preparing and enjoying these meals, and we sincerely hope that you will have the same experience as you recreate them in your camp or home.

14

The Hobo Pack

A ground beef hobo pack

The first meal I ever learned to cook at camp was the Hobo Pack, meat, vegetables, and seasoning wrapped in foil and tossed into the fire. In the 80s, my parents would take us camping for weeks at a time in Southern Indiana, and they would have my siblings and me in an assembly line making up our foil packs. We loved it. This remains one of my favorite meals to eat because they are so versatile and delicious. Any meat can be used; ground beef and chicken are the most used, but I have done fish, lamb, and various other questionable meats

49

successfully. I could make this entire book about Hobo pack varieties, so just understand there are no limits to this simple cooking technique.

Ingredients

- Salt & pepper
- Garlic powder or cloves
- 1 Onion, sliced
- 1 Chicken Breast or Burger Patty
- 1 Potato, sliced
- Handful of Vegetables of choice (broccoli, carrots, peppers, etc.)
- ¼ stick of butter
- Aluminum foil

Steps

Lay out the foil, roughly 18-24" long. Place your chosen meat upon it and season it heavily. Place sliced/chopped vegetables of choice around the meat and season those with salt, pepper, and garlic to taste. Place pads of butter evenly around the dish. Now, wrap the contents in the foil. Wrap in at least three layers of foil; use additional sheets as needed. Then toss into a campfire, not the middle, but the edge, for 30-45 minutes. Check with a meat thermometer or cut a slit to check on meat and to see if vegetables are burning too much. It's very common for charred potatoes and vegetables to be along the foil edges. You can also cook these in an oven or casserole dish the same way at 350 degrees for 60-70 minutes on average.

Serve from the foil; just cut a slit and open it up!

Students preparing Hobo meals

A finished Hobo Pack

15

Kentucky Fried Squirrel

Fried Squirrel cooked on the Coleman stove.

I grew up on fried squirrel. I recall many days when my dad would bring back a handful of "grays," which would set the house to hop in anticipation of the meal. This dish is a staple in my region, and this recipe keeps it simple.

Ingredients

- 1 Squirrel, cut up
- 1 c. All-purpose flour
- seasoned salt
- 1 egg
- Pepper to taste
- 2 T. milk
- Vegetable Oil

Steps

Mix the flour, pepper, and seasoned salt on a plate. Mix egg and milk in a bowl. Dip pieces of the cut-up squirrel in the egg mixture, then roll them into the flour mixture just like you would chicken. Preheat your vegetable oil in a skillet (cast iron preferred). Place the coated squirrel pieces into hot oil until golden brown. Remove from oil, place in a Dutch oven or roasting pan, and bake for an hour at 275 degrees. *You may also prepare rabbits this way.

16

Squirrel & Dumplings

A delicious one-pot meal option that permits you the freedom to roam around for the day while the food is cooking.

Ingredients

- 2 squirrels 2 stalks of celery chopped
- 2 T Vegetable oil 4 carrots, sliced then chopped
- 1 T butter (salted) 2 T. cornstarch (thickener)
- 3 c. water
- 1 tsp. salt
- ¼ tsp. pepper
- 1 Onion, sliced (I prefer Vidalia's)

Dumplings:

- 1 c. flour ½ c. milk
- 2 tsp. baking powder 2 T. Salad oil (any oil)
- ½ tsp. salt

Steps

Cut the squirrels into serving-size pieces and brown them in oil and butter in a Dutch oven before adding water, salt, and pepper. Simmer over medium heat for around 30-40 minutes to desired tenderness. Add vegetables and water if needed and cook for 20 more minutes; thicken the mixture with the cornstarch and 2T water premixed, then add to the pot.

Prepare your dumplings by sifting all ingredients together, then add milk and oil and stir until a dough is formed. Drop your dumpling dough by the tablespoon on top of the boiling stew. Place on low heat or move next to the cooking fire and allow to simmer for 15 minutes-do not lift the cover during this time! Be patient and let the magic happen. Your dumplings will plump and solidify enough to serve with your fantastic stew. *Again, rabbits, game fouls, or chickens can also be prepared this way.

Raccoon BBQ

Shredded Raccoon BBQ, ready for sauce
Prepared by John Dosch

Ingredients

- 1 Racoon
- 1 bottle of fruit juice (Pineapple, Apple, or Orange)
- 1 Bottle BBQ Sauce of choice
- Salt & pepper to taste
- Optional: Bacon

Steps

Process your raccoon by removing as much fat as possible (keep it for other uses as desired). I soak mine after processing in a saltwater bath, changing the water every few hours until it's no longer pink (removing as much blood as I can from the meat). I then quarter the raccoon and place it in a Dutch oven, covering it with the fruit juice and an entire bottle of BBQ sauce. I add water as needed to cover the meat, then bring it to a boil and allow it to cook until the meat falls from the bone. You will need to add water to this dish as it boils off. Just enough to keep the meat covered until done to the desired tenderness.

Preparing to braise the Raccoon with bacon in the Dutch Oven

If you have added too much water, you may need to drain the meat. The remaining juices can be used as a wet dressing for the meat, or you can discard them for fresh BBQ sauce as desired—salt and pepper to taste. I hit mine with a broiler or toss it back into the oven to dry it out and get some "outside brown" (crispy edges). This serves well with your standard BBQ fares such as coleslaw and baked beans but can also be served over rice or with sweet potatoes. *You may cook raccoons any way you think to cook a beef roast.

18

Possum Fricassee

Generally, I do not recommend eating opossums due to their scavenging nature. That said, "possum" has been a mainstay dish of the old south for generations, and I have certainly prepared my fair share of the critters at many camps. I've served this Creole-inspired version a few times to rave reviews.

Ingredients

- 1 Opossum
- 1 stick of butter
- 1 large onion
- 2 c. water
- 1 large can of peaches
- Sourdough Bread
- 2 sweet potatoes
- Smoked Sausage Link
- 1 T. Garlic Powder
- Salt and pepper to taste

Possum, sweet potatoes, and onions prepared for cooking

Steps

Prepare possum by carefully cleaning the meat and soaking it in saltwater, changing the water every couple of hours until clear. Slice onion and potatoes. Place meat into a Dutch oven, season with garlic powder, salt, and pepper, then top with onion and potatoes. Then, add in the can of peaches, including the juice. Slice the butter into pads and evenly distribute the butter around the dish and add 2 cups of water.

I like to cook this low and slow; possum cooks like pork for the most part. Regularly baste the meat and turn the ingredients, so everything gets ample opportunity to become the fricassee gravy. Once the meat is done, remove from heat, cook your sourdough loaf in a reflector oven, and cook your sausage links over the fire until the skins burst and are heated throughout. Serve the possum with the potatoes, onions, and any peach leftovers you find. Cover the dish with the drippings and add some rustic bread slices and the fire-cooked sausage links for the Creole-inspired dish.

19

Coyote Chili

Coyote Chili

Authentic chili (chili con carne) originated not in Texas but Spain. 17th-century nun Sister Mary of Agreda penned the first recipe. The Spanish then brought it to San Antonio as the Spanish Catholics began to settle in the region, thus birthing what we now know as Texas Chili, later Cowboy Chili. I grew up in Southern Indiana, where chili is tomato soup with chili seasoning, hamburger, spaghetti noodles, and some chili beans. It's watery and, well, soup, not chili (sorry, Grandma). Thankfully, my dad, born in Memphis and brought up around the pit BBQ scene due to his father's involvement in the food industry, was an educated foodie instructed from a young age in the proper ways of chili and Pit BBQ, which he passed on to me. All jesting aside, please prepare the chili according to your preferred method; I'll provide my basic recipe here.

The author processing coyote meat

Ingredients

- 2lb Coyote Meat, cubed (similar to skirt steak) - or any meat you have!
- 1 Large Onion
- 2 Cans Rotel Tomatoes with Green Chilis
- 2 Boxes of Jiffy Corn Muffin Mix

Chili Seasoning:

- 1/3 c. chili powder
- 1/2 tsp. cumin
- 2 tsp. Oregano
- 2 tsp. smoked paprika
- 2 tsp. salt
- 3 tsp. minced garlic
- (Alternatively, use 2 Packets of store-bought Chili Season)

Optional:

- 1-2 16oz can(s) of chili or kidney beans (a good way to stretch servings)
- 1 can of tomato sauce
- Sliced Jalapeno
- Sour Cream
- Shredded Cheese

Steps

In a Dutch oven, cook your meat and season with salt and pepper or the seasoning of your choice. When cooking coyote, we only use the thigh or external loin to avoid opening the gut cavity. Coyote meat should be carefully cleaned, inspected, and soaked with repeated salt-water changes until clean. You should cook it thoroughly. Chop your onion. Remove the cooked meat from heat, drain the grease, then add your chili seasoning ingredients. Stir thoroughly, then add the Rotel cans of tomatoes and chopped onion. If you desire optional components, such as beans, add them now.

Simmer for 30 minutes and stir. Add water to the Jiffy Corn Muffin mixes to create the batter according to the directions. Remove the lid from the Dutch oven and pour batter on top of the chili, then replace the lid and keep on low heat until the Jiffy mix turns golden brown and cooks through (generally 30 minutes). Once cooked, you will have cornbread with your chili from the same Dutch oven; top with shredded cheese, sliced jalapeno, and sour cream as desired.

Corn mix cooked on top of chili.

20

Roasted Goat

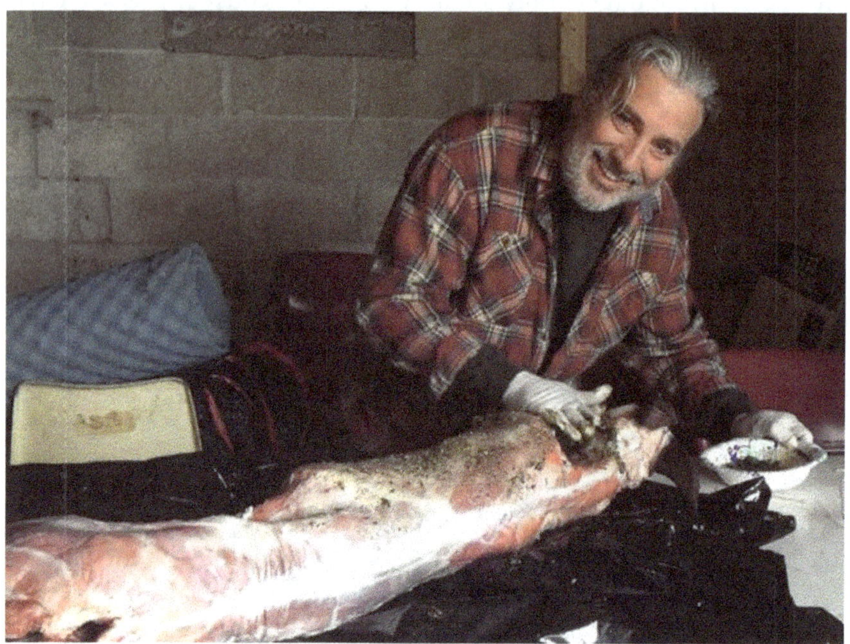

Greg, massaging a goat with oils and spices

While goats may not be high on your list of available camp meats, deer likely are. Deer, sheep, and goats are all delicate meats that share many of the same recipe profiles. A small deer or sheep roasted in this manner would be a big hit at the next camp and is a wonderful way to celebrate the Biblical Passover as we do with friends and family every Spring. This recipe is one we used for a large Passover dinner while at camp.

66

Ingredients

Amounts will vary depending on the size of the animal.

- Whole goat
- Olive Oil
- Sea Salt
- Cracked Pepper
- Rosemary
- Garlic Cloves
- 2-3 sticks of butter

Create a paste of olive oil, salt, pepper, garlic cloves, and rosemary in a dish. Poke holes into the carcass in meaty areas to insert whole cloves of garlic (the number will depend on the animal's size). Coat the animal in the paste, then run a spit through the animal, making sure it's secure so you can rotate the spit as needed. Once the meat is over a bed of cooking coals, lay 1/4" pads of butter upon the top of the meat. The butter will melt as the meat cooks, and once fully melted, rotate the meat and place additional pads of butter on top again and repeat this process until the meat has been fully coated in a layer of butter as it cooks. Any remaining butter can be mixed with the remaining seasoning to be used as a baste while the meat finishes cooking. Once done, serve right off the spit!

Roasted Goat secured to spit

21

Chicken Pot Pie

One day at camp, we all started discussing the problems with chicken pot pies. We all loved the concept and had yet to find one that we could unanimously agree that was good and didn't taste like cardboard. The debate just made me hungry for one, so as the commentary continued, I started cooking and came up with this version of a pot pie that I surprised the team with. Everyone was pleased with it as it addressed all the problems without the cardboard flavor. I have also cooked this with wild turkey, and the results were even better.

Ingredients

- 4-6 boneless/skinless chicken breasts, chopped
- Canadian Chicken season (Montreal season)
- 1lb bag of frozen mixed vegetables (peas, carrots)
- 2 cans of cream of chicken (or 1 large can)
- Water (as needed)
- 2 cans of biscuits (flaky variety)
- Salt and pepper

Steps

In a Dutch oven, cook the chicken and season with the Canadian chicken blend. I use an above-average amount of seasoning to some degree to permeate the vegetables. Once the chicken is cooked, add frozen vegetables and chicken stock. Thin the mixture with water as desired. I usually add 1 can of water (8-12oz) to thin it out. Mix well and add some salt and pepper. Now, cook until vegetables are done, usually 8-10 minutes. I generally bring the mixture to a low boil for several minutes, mixing it regularly to prevent burning on the bottom. Once piping hot, remove the lid and lay the biscuits out over the top of the mixture. Stacking the last one or two biscuits, if needed, is okay, so long as they do not touch the top of the lid. Replace the lid and add coals to the top and bottom of the oven to finish cooking the biscuits. Once the biscuits are golden brown, the meal is ready to serve.

Polynesian Chicken

**Chicken cooked inside a
watermelon**

I stumbled across this idea when preparing for a Coastal Survival class in the Florida Keys. I wanted to share something new and different. I learned of watermelons being used as cooking vessels in India, and they would hollow them out and put holes all over them to hang chicken within the melon. I thought, why not just use it like a Dutch oven, so I tried it. My first attempt resulted in a melon that disintegrated in the fire- I had to dig out the chicken, which was still amazing. In subsequent attempts, I wrapped the melon in foil and began achieving outstanding results!

Ingredients

- 1 medium size Watermelon
- 4-6 Chicken Breasts or any game bird chunked up
- 1-2 c. Long Grain & Wild Rice Blend (Any Rice)
- 1 can of Pineapple Chunks
- 1 bottle of Teriyaki sauce
- Salt & pepper
- Cheesecloth or shemagh
- 4-5 Bamboo Skewers (Spike sticks)
- Aluminum Foil

Steps

Cut just shy of the top third of the watermelon off. Hollow the watermelon, leaving enough pulp inside to cover the white rind. Take the remaining watermelon pulp and set it inside your cheesecloth or shemagh and squeeze out roughly 1-2 cups of watermelon juice, commensurate with the rice you plan to cook. Save any leftover watermelon to enjoy as a garnish. Place 1/2 cup of rice in the bottom of the watermelon. Coat your chicken with salt, pepper, and teriyaki sauce in another dish. Layer the chicken inside the melon atop the rice, and pour any remaining teriyaki sauce over the chicken.

Separate the pineapple chunks from the liquid in the can, but save the liquid. Place the pineapple pieces atop and around the chicken. Cover the chicken with the remaining rice, and pour the pineapple and watermelon juice over the rice. Place the top back on the melon and use the skewers to pin it securely to the top. Wrap the melon in at least three layers of aluminum foil. Place the covered melon into your fire and allow it to cook for 50-60 minutes. You can use a meat thermometer to pierce the side of the melon through the foil to check the chicken's temperature; otherwise, open the melon to check that the rice has hydrated and the chicken has cooked through. Wrap it back up and cook an additional twenty minutes at a time until done. The rice will have a sweet hint of watermelon and pineapple, and the chicken will be moist with a light glaze- delicious!

Lightly glazed Polynesian Chicken

23

Pit Cooked Ropa Vieja

Pit Cooked Roast

I love Cuban food and try to eat it often. One dish we have adopted in our camps is Ropa Vieja, a Spanish dish adopted by the Cuban people and means "old clothes" or "shredded rope." The story goes that a poor man had no food for his family, so he shredded his clothes and cooked them in a pot, and after praying, the clothes turned into shredded meat. Instead of a pot, we're using a pit for cooking the meat. Pit cooking is very easy and requires little preparation. You can dig a pit, make a fire in it for about an hour, then drop your meat in it to be cooked- or you can preheat the ground and move the fire to dig into the hot ground. The results are the same. If you are new to this cooking method, start digging a hole roughly three times the size of the meat you plan to cook. Start a fire in the hole and establish a solid coal bed. Once a coal bed is established, lay your foil-wrapped meat on it, adding kindling around the outside and on top of it. Allow it to catch fire, then bury it in the soil. Depending on the size of the meat you choose to cook, 3-5 hours is a general idea of how long it takes to cook this way. If you find you cannot pull the bone from the meat yet, stoke the fire in the hole and bury it for an additional hour or more as needed.

Ingredients

- Beef, Lamb, or Pork Roast
- Olive or Avacado Oil
- Fruit Juice
- Mojo Seasoning (oregano, cumin, garlic, onion, black pepper, and jalapeno.)
- 1-2 Onions
- 2-3 Bell Peppers
- 1 can of Coconut water or Pina Colada Soda
- Rice
- Black Beans

Steps

Prepare the roast by scoring a few lines in the meat for marinade and spices. Soak the roast in fruit juice such as Orange, Apple, or

Grapefruit juice for a couple of hours before cooking. This will break down the meat fibers and soften the tissue. Lightly coat the roast with oil, then rub the dry Mojo seasoning all over it before wrapping it in at least three layers of foil. You may add a splash of juice to the meat inside the foil if you think it's needed. In a prepared pit, set the meat fat side down. Once buried, allow 3-5 hours to cook.

Pit and Dish Cooked Chicken with Rice cooked in bamboo in Florida Keys

About an hour before the meat is finished, prepare the side dishes. Dice the onions, add to the black beans, and allow to simmer until the meat is done. Slice the bell peppers and remaining onion into slices and caramelize in a skillet with a splash of fruit juice and a pinch of salt. Cook your rice with coconut water or pina colada soda. We use a Pina Colada energy drink for the caffeine energy boost when we have a late night ahead.

Once the meat is finished, open the foil and shred the meat; any bones should easily pull away. Serve the bell peppers and onions on top of the meat (if you like it that way) with the rice and beans on the sides.

24

Greg's Swamp Cabbage

Swamp cabbage is an old-time Florida dish. Having lived in Florida for the greater part of my life, I was influenced by regional cuisine. The Old-Timer that influenced my version of this dish was "Paw," the owner of People's Ranch in Southwest Florida. Paw narrates his life during the intro to the Zack Brown Band video "Same Boat." He recently passed, and with him, countless great tales of a childhood and subsistence life in rural Florida were left to his son Jimmy aka "Huntin Buddy." Here's to keeping the rural traditions alive.

Ingredients

- The tender inner trunk of a cabbage palm/sabal palm with nearly equal parts

- Tomatoes. You can use canned diced tomatoes if you don't have fresh ones.
- Okra sliced into bite-size pieces
- Salt and pepper to taste.
- Water as needed to make a stew consistency
- Seafood of choice (clams, shrimp, crab, snapper, rockfish, etc.)
- Rice (Optional)
- Hot Sauce (Optional)

Steps

In a non-aluminum cook pot or Dutch Oven, boil the above ingredients until the swamp cabbage is tender, about 15 minutes. The okra will help thicken the stew, so be ready to add a little water at this point. Add seafood of your choice. I've used shrimp, clams, crab meat, chunks of snapper, grouper, and rockfish. Cook another five to ten minutes. Don't overcook the seafood! Serve by itself or over steamed rice. Add hot sauce if you like.

25

Roast Beef Hash

This recipe I was treated to during a Bushcraft gathering created by Jamie Burleigh. It was so good I came home and made it for my family, and it's since become a regular meal we enjoy any time of the day.

Ingredients

- 4 cans of Roast Beef Hash (Corned beef works too)
- 6 eggs
- 1 onion, diced*
- 1 tomato, diced*
- Sour cream (optional)
- Salsa (optional)
- Cheese (optional)

* Pico de Gallo makes a wonderful alternative

Heat the hash in a skillet until a light crust is formed on the bottom. Attempt to flip the hash patty over in the skillet in one piece; otherwise, continue to brown as uniformly as possible to establish a light crust layer. Crack eggs over the hash, evenly spaced, and allow to cook through. Cover with remaining ingredients and serve.

26

The Hobbit Pot

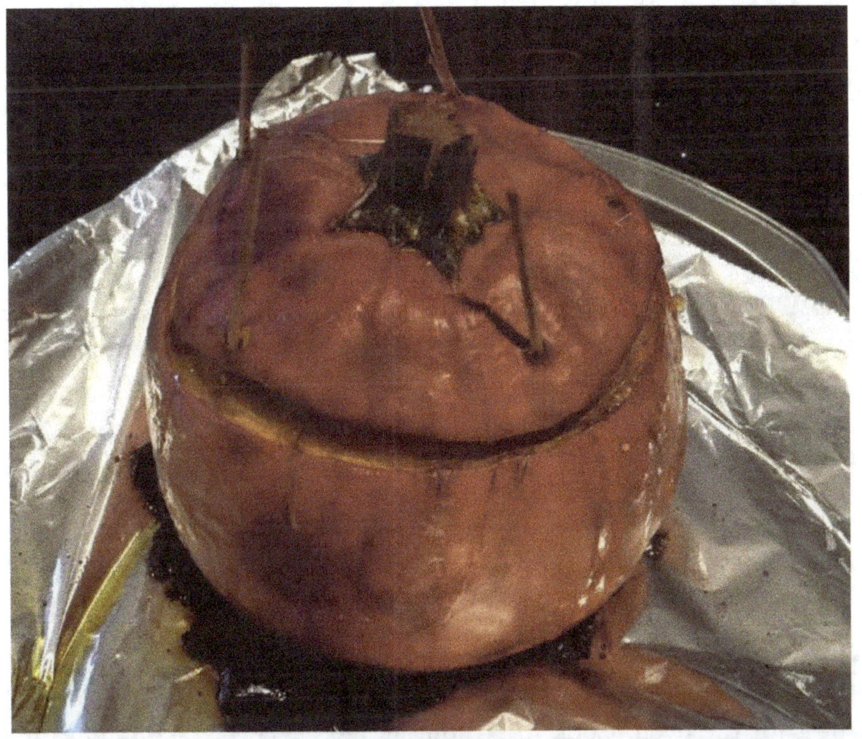

Cooked Hobbit Pot

After making the Polynesian Chicken in the watermelon, I figured I could just as likely make a thanksgiving dinner in a pumpkin. Greg Laughlin, an instructor with our school, beat me to it and created this dish we call *The Hobbit Pot*. It looks like something you would roll from

83

a Hobbit hole deep in the forest. It's easy to make and sticks to the ribs. Try this one this fall; it can be made in the oven or at the campfire.

Ingredients:

- 1 Pumpkin (size depends on how many will eat)
- Quinoa and Wild Rice (Any rice)
- Turkey or Chicken, or a 50/50 Ground Beef/Sausage Pork mixture
- 1 stick of Butter, softened
- Salt & pepper
- Allspice or Cinnamon & Sugar
- ½ c. Thinly Sliced Potatoes or Hash Browns
- Aluminum Foil
- Skewers

Steps

Cut the top off the pumpkin and remove the pulp. You can save the seeds for later roasting. Once clear, mix the all-spice or cinnamon and sugar with a pinch of salt with half the stick of softened butter. Mix well, and coat the pumpkin's interior by hand (yes, it's messy). Once covered, place sliced potatoes or hashbrowns at the bottom 1/4th, stack meat on top, then rice blend on top of the meat. Add remaining butter with ½ cup of water. Place the lid onto the pumpkin and use at least four skewers to pin it into place. Now, wrap the pumpkin in at least three layers of foil if campfire cooking, or place it on a foil-lined baking sheet for the oven. Cook for 1 hour at 350 degrees or 45 minutes in an active campfire, then check the contents with a meat thermometer or crack it open to examine. Spoon out as desired, or slice and serve for a rustic plate deserving of the woods. Add additional seasoning as desired.

Sliced open and ready to eat

Rotisserie Chicken

We often hand out cornish hens to students to cook for themselves during winter classes. It's a great way for people to bond with their teammates and learn about camp cooking and fire management. Jamie Burleigh, an instructor at our school, had the great idea to add multiple spears through our chicken so that it could be rotated in nearly every configuration. The moistest and most delicious rotisserie chicken we have had to date resulted from the experiment, and it has set the standard for all others to follow since. We prepared a wooden tripod, lashed a platform to it at 1/3rd of the height, perfect for cooking on, then placed two cross sticks in a V formation atop the platform. A center spit was run through the chicken with two shorter spits through the sides, front and back. This configuration allowed it to be cooked equally on its sides, top, and bottom. The golden brown skin speaks for itself- it was truly delicious and the envy of the camp.

Chicken cooking on the tripod

Ingredients

- 1 Chicken, skin on
- Cooking Oil (we used vegetable oil)
- Garlic Mustard, Wild Onion Finely Chopped (or Canadian Chicken season)
- Salt & Pepper to taste

Steps

Place chicken onto spits, then coat with oil. Apply chopped herbs and spices to the oiled chicken, and begin to cook. Rotate into a new position every 10-minutes and follow up with a light glaze of oil until done. Skin will be golden brown and crispy. Total cook time averages 60-90 minutes, depending on the fire.

28

Whatya Got Pot

The Whatya Got Pot is usually done when no one can decide what to eat, so you just see what everyone has, then toss it into the pot. I have never had this one go bad yet, and it's a very convenient way to make a hearty one-pot meal. There's not a recipe for this per se, but there are a few guidelines I try to follow.

Guidelines

- Don't mix meats: Beef, pork, and chicken; raccoon, groundhog, and venison all cook differently, so to avoid any potential upset stomachs, I choose one meat for the pot and cook others separately. This is, of course, unless we end up with a food profile that warrants mixing meats or using complimentary meats, such as in Fajitas, where I would cook the steak, chicken, and peppers together, or in chili, I would cook beef and raccoon together. Once the meats are cooked, I have no problem mixing them later. This little thing makes me feel safer feeding strangers and allows people more options to test the wild game before going all in.
- Try to add in a contribution from everyone: If you can include whatever someone hands you, it makes them feel better and adds to the pot, which goes a long way in boosting morale and

can serve as a teaching moment if you find they brought Brussel sprouts to camp without a plan to use them (It happens a lot).

- If it's questionable, use it anyway: In a one-pot meal, you boil the contents for an extended period. So things that may appear too soggy, limp, or maybe sat in the cooler a day longer than they should have are generally okay to use. However, anything molded or with a putrid odor should be discarded.
- Season heavily: Salt, Pepper, Garlic, or whatever anyone has; be generous with it.
- Fruit juice for the win: A heavy shot or a bottle of fruit juice with citric acid will do wonders for breaking down tough meats and flavoring your meal.
- Bread always: Reflector oven bread is always a hit at camp. You can use Take and Bake varieties to make life easier and work faster for yourself, but when using the Whatya Got Pot, the bread will make up for mealtime blunders.

Random items, and Brussel sprouts in the Dutch oven

29

Coal Cooked Squirrel

This is not a recipe but a cooking method you likely have not tried. Jamie Burleigh shared this with me, a technique he has been sharing with the Indigenous people of Canada, where he's accepted as a skills instructor. Squirrel hides are tough, and these are one of only a few animals you can do this with that are common in the United States. With this method, you do not need a knife, and you do not remove the animal's entrails. Once a good bed of coals is established, you simply toss the squirrel on the fire to singe off the hair, then bury it in the coals. Flip it a few times during cooking until the front claws fall off, which is the sign that it's done cooking.

Brush off the ash and pull on the leg, which should come off easily and be ready to enjoy. The animal's innards tighten into a clump and will pop out with the flick of a stick. If available, continue to cook any leftover meat and bones in a pot to create a bone broth. This cooking technique is one that Indigenous people have used for millennia, and we don't want it lost to history, especially since it's a viable method a woodsman can use in a survival situation.

30

Howlers

A long-time friend and patron of our school, Kevin Baxter, entered this recipe in our Bushcraft Master Chef challenge some years ago; they were an immediate hit. In a short time, we started using them and versions of them as a treat for late-night camps. While teaching, we often waited for students to finish nighttime navigation courses. While most students were in the field, instructors would remain in camp, keeping fires stoked and testing students as they returned. Some groups would take many hours to complete the courses as we didn't have strict time limits in the early days, which was a mistake. Howlers kept us motivated to pull those 4 am shifts as we ventured into the dark woods to find what was holding up students with navigational impairments.

Howlers filling a 17" Lodge Skillet

Ingredients

- 1lb Bacon
- 1 Package Sausage links (Hot links, Italian, or Polish)
- Shredded Cheese

Steps

In a cast iron skillet, brown and split the sausage links, so they become crispy. Remove from heat, add shredded cheese to the split side, then wrap with bacon. Move back onto the fire. Once the bacon is cooked, you can cover it with more cheese as desired. Then serve- an easy and tasty treat anytime you're afield.

Fiesta Shepherd's Pie

Shepherd's Pie has its origin in the sheep herding highlands of Scotland. It's essentially a casserole with layers of meat and vegetables topped with mashed potatoes, and sometimes cheese baked until a light crust is formed. My wife, Robyn, found a spin on the dish for a camp once that became one of our most requested dishes from returning students, the Fiesta Shepherd's Pie. Being short of mixed vegetables, she opted for taco seasoning and chili beans and it resulted in a delicious Tex-Mex flavor combination, which she followed up with some Jalapeno corn muffins.

Ingredients

- 1lb ground beef
- 1 packet of taco seasoning
    - do not add oil or water to seasoning
- 1 can of chili beans
- 1 can (11 oz) fiesta corn
- 1pouch loaded mashed potatoes
    - Water, milk, and butter called for on the potatoes pouch
- 1/2 c. shredded Cheddar cheese (2 oz)
- 1/2 c. chopped green onion

Steps

Brown ground beef, drain the grease, and add taco seasoning. Mix in fiesta corn and chili beans and simmer on medium heat, occasionally stirring while you prepare the mashed potatoes. Prepare potatoes according to the directions on the packet, then remove the meat mixture from heat and spoon the mashed potatoes over top of the meat. Cover the dish with cheese and heat in a Dutch oven until cheese melts. Garnish with chopped onions.

This dish serves well with tortilla chips- especially those you make fresh in camp by frying tortilla shells. But, we usually serve it with Jiffy Corn mix muffins. Follow the directions on the box, then add in your own fresh chopped jalapeno. If you have a large group, make it in a casserole and add 1/2 c. of sour cream, 1 can of whole corn, and 1 can of creamed corn. This will make a thick and heart corn muffin cake that is wonderful served alongside the pie.

32

Stuffed Peppers

Stuffed peppers are another campfire treat that many will enjoy. I always wondered why no one I ever camped with served stuffed peppers, so I showed up with some to a class I was teaching and showed them how easy it was to do it. Keep in mind that I had never done it myself-but I understood the concept, having done it at home many times.

Ingredients

- 1lb Jalapeno Peppers (or pepper of choice)
- 1lb Ground Italian Sausage (Hot, mild, or sweet)
- 1lb Bacon
- 2 blocks Cream Cheese
- Shredded cheese

Fire roasted stuffed peppers

Steps

Slice peppers lengthwise, removing any seeds, then char the peppers. You want actual charring or brown spots on the peppers. As this is cooking, cook the sausage in a cast iron skillet. Chop as you cook to crumble it and get slight crispiness to the sausage. Drain grease, then add in cream cheese and allow to melt; fold sausage and cream cheese together until it's well mixed. The peppers and sausage should be ready within minutes of each other; set them to the side, and begin cooking bacon to desired crispness.

Spoon in sausage mixture to peppers; you may just smear it across, then lay a slice of bacon overtop. Finish by using shredded cheese as a topping and place back over the fire to melt cheese, then serve.

33

Grilled Heart

Heart! Yes, it does not sound appetizing, but it is one of the most delicious cuts of meat you will find. Greg first had this recipe in a remote resort outside Lima, Peru. As he tells it: Jorge, the cook, was making "pinchos", small skewers of grilled meats and seafood as a snack around the bar he was tending. As I watched him, he noted my interest and offered to show me how he made the spice rub. The heart was never a favorite of mine since I found it to always taste like iron or, well, like a heart.

This rub changed all that. I like to serve this as a snack or as a meal adding grilled or fried sweet potatoes or yucca fries. Feel free to adjust the chili-based spices according to your level of heat. Don't skip the achiote if you can find it. Any Hispanic foods section of a grocery store usually has some if it's not in the spice section. Sometimes it's called Annato seed.

We have made this around the fire using beef, deer, and lamb heart with excellent results. Campers usually find it so good that there's none left over for the chef.

Ingredients

- 1 whole heart
- 2 T. oregano
- 2 tsp ground cumin
- 4 T. (mix of achiote seeds, paprika, chili powder, and cayenne)
- 4 or more garlic cloves; I mash the achiote seeds and garlic in a mortar and pestle
- 1 cup red wine or apple cider vinegar
- 1 cup canola oil
- Wooden skewers soaked in water

Steps

Cut the heart into one-inch cubes and place them in a bowl with all the ingredients. Mix well to incorporate and let marinate for 2-4 hrs. Remove meat and place on a paper towel to let the excess oil drain off. Insert four pieces onto each skewer and grill over a fire for three to four minutes, basting with leftover liquid. Serve hot off the grill.

Bonus- that flavorful marinade hitting the hot coals will create the most delicious-smelling smoke and make the most reluctant campers come running for a taste.

34

Trail Pasty

A Pasty is a baked pastry stuffed with meat, potatoes, and vegetables. Miners from Cornwall, England, brought the first pasty recipes with them as they began working in the upper peninsula region of Michigan to mine copper. Finnish miners and workers that settled in the region adopted these quickly as they served them well in the mines for days at a time. These have long been the portable meals of the Northwoods, and with a simple hack, you can easily create these in camp to hand out to everyone before a long day afield. If I'm going hunting all day, I'll carry one of these in my haversack along with a small cheese and smattering of jerky. This recipe will make six pasties.

Ingredients

8oz Ground beef, but any meat of choice will work

1 Carrot, diced into 1/4" pieces

1 Onion, diced into 1/4" pieces

1 Potato, diced into 1/4" pieces

1 egg, whisked

Hack #1: Use a bag of frozen diced hashbrowns with pepper and onion blend and a bag of frozen diced carrots.

Salt and Pepper to taste

Hack #2: Instead of making pastry in camp, use two 8oz sheets of crescent dough in the biscuit section of your local grocer.

Steps:

Cook the meat, potatoes, and vegetables in a pot until done. Season to taste. Set aside the mixture, then lay out the dough on a flat surface, and spoon a generous amount of the meat mixture into six piles on the dough. Take the second sheet of dough and lay it on the other, making the top cover of the pasty. Cut to shape according to the piles (Traditional D shape or Rectangles), then use a fork to press closed the edges of the pie. Cut 2-3 tiny slits on top of each pie, just enough for moisture to escape, then brush each with the whisked egg wash. You can then bake at 350 degrees in a preheated oven on a baking sheet or reflector oven according to the crescent dough instructions, or Hack #3; you can deep dry them. Both ways taste great; you can freeze these and reheat them as desired (300 degrees for 20 minutes). Great for cold weather camping and anytime you need a handy pocket meal.

Reflector oven Pasties

35

The Mob Boss

This was another late-night recipe we stumbled into while trying to use up the remaining ingredients we had in the cooler. We find this to be amazing when cooked in a Dutch oven, especially if you want more consistent cheese caramelization. Onions make this extra special too. However, wrapped in foil, it's a hit every time we've made it.

Ingredients

- 2 Provolone Cheese Slices

- 12 Pepperoni Slices
- 1 Chicken Breast
- Italian Dressing
- Foil or a Dutch Oven

Steps

On your foil or in the oven, lay down the cheese slices. If using cast iron, I recommend laying down pads of butter before the cheese (you'll thank me later). Lay pepperoni on the cheese, then chicken, and coat it with Italian dressing. Wrap in at least three layers of foil. You can put it at the edge of a fire to cook until the chicken is done, then serve. If you use the Dutch oven method, the drippings from this can be used as a dip for Bannock/bread or marinade for another meal.

36

Polish Hunter's Stew

According to Greg, this stew evokes images of the bearded Hunter braving a chilly, misty fall morning, walking the field edges and hedgerows harvesting the small game this land offers. His weathered and worn shotgun is ready, cradled in the crook of his elbow as he patiently walks alone or perhaps in the company of his faithful hound. Feel free to go rogue with this recipe, use whatever small game your woods offer, and enjoy this around the campfire or by the wood stove with your hunting partners. As a Buffalo, NY native, he grew up experiencing heavy snows, cold winters, and a thriving Polish community.

Ingredients

- 6 T Crisco or rendered fat
- 1 rabbit jointed then quartered
- Several game birds
    - I use approx 4 quail halved and grouse, pheasant, or Cornish hens, broken down into the leg, thigh, and breast portions
- 1lb of thick-cut bacon
- 2 large carrots diced
- 2 large white or yellow onions
- 1lb sauerkraut
- 2 oz dried mushrooms (rehydrated in a pint of hot water and reserved)
- 4 plum tomatoes chopped (or a can of diced)
- 3 bay leaves
- 2 tsp thyme
- 2 tsp caraway seeds
- 1 tsp crushed juniper berries
- 3 c. of bone or veg stock
- 1 c. of red wine or dark beer
- 1/2lb smoked Polish sausage. ** cut into bite-size pieces

- 12oz of frozen potato gnocchi or make your version (dumplings)

**Greg grew up with Wardynski's Polish sausage (with marjoram!), a Buffalo, NY staple for four generations. Wardynski.com **

Steps

Heat fat and add the bacon to render. Add game a few pieces at a time, season as you go, frying meat in the fat. Remove the game and set aside; add onions and carrots and stir until onions are translucent and soft. Add sauerkraut and continue to stir occasionally, mixing vegetables. Add game meat to the pot with mushrooms and their liquid, tomatoes, herbs, spices, stock/wine, etc.

Cover and simmer for 45min checking to ensure the pan doesn't go dry. Add sausage and adjust seasoning as needed. Simmer about 45 additional minutes. The game meat should be shredding and falling off the bone.

Add potato gnocchi and stir throughout to combine.

Serve in a bowl with some crusty bread alongside your favorite camp beverage. As they say in Poland, "Schnitz Smacznego!"

Snacks, Sides, and Desserts

"Cooking and eating food outdoors makes it taste infinitely better than the same meal prepared and consumed indoors."
-- Fennel Hudson, "Fine Things - Fennel's Journal - No. 8."

A proper camp meal cannot be complete without snacks, side dishes, or desserts. These make great anytime snack options and treats to boost camp morale, take a break for fellowship, and add that extra kick to round out a wonderful camp dinner.

37

Mom's Dump Cobbler

Look at those edges!

Jason's mom makes some of the best cobblers and has mastered caramelizing them along the edges, so you get the perfect balance of crispy goodness and moistness. This recipe can take just about any fruit and make an amazing cobbler. I usually go for peaches or pears, but I've also made blackberry, raspberry, and cherry. During a stretch of classes, I forgot to grab the fruit on more than one occasion, but we were able to forage for local berries, including autumn olive one time, to create an amazing cobbler all the same.

Ingredients
1 c. flour
1 c. sugar
1 c. milk
½ stick of butter (or entire stick)
16oz of fruit
Optional: Brown sugar

Steps
My mom used to dump all the ingredients, give them one stir and cook it. This is the dump method, and it works just fine, and I recommend you try it this way. I like to refine mine a little more because I usually cook for many people at a camp, so I want my ingredients to be more evenly distributed.

In a 10" cast iron skillet, pour flour, milk, and sugar to make a batter. I like to whisk the batter, but it's not necessary. If your skillet is not well seasoned, first coat it in butter before making the batter. After the batter, pour in the fruit, distribute evenly, then cook at 350 degrees for 45-60 minutes. I like to hit with a dash of brown sugar during the last several minutes of cooking for a little color and pop. Allow to cool before serving- goes perfectly with camp-made ice cream.

38

Breads for the Woods

Bushpot Bannock

Bannock has been a staple of woodmen for centuries. Nothing makes a meal better than warm bread while afield. Here are a handful of ways that Jamie has prepared bannocks for us around various camps over the years.

Ingredients

- 1 cup flour
- 1 tsp. baking powder
- dash salt
- 1/3 c. water
- Single serving recipe/ 1=palm-sized loaf

Bisquick Bannock Modern Standby

- 6-8 tablespoons of water
- 1 cup Bisquick buttermilk baking mix

Flatten it out into a cake, about 1/2 inch thick, and fry it in a little oil, very slowly over coals or the lowest possible flame. Fry it as gently as possible, turning it often. After the bottom is browned, prop the pan before the fire's flames to brown the top.

Pro-tips: The batter should not be too thick - 1/2 inch is enough. Use a straight-sided fry pan; curved sides allow slips when propped before the fire. Aluminum skillets get too hot too quickly; avoid them. Don't prop up the pan until the bottom is browned.

Steam Baked Bannock Bread

Put the dough in a zip-lock freezer bag. Place it on a rack over a pot of boiling water. Let the steam 'bake' the bread. Add raisins and cinnamon, or serve with honey.

Stick or "Twisty" bread, an old-time favorite

Ingredients

- 1 cup Bisquick mix
- water
- cinnamon and sugar

Steps

Mix the Bisquick with enough water to form a dough. Roll into a long piece and wrap or twist around a clean green stick (not dried out). Sprinkle cinnamon sugar on a twist. Place or hold a stick over a fire and bake on all sides. Bake until golden brown. Break off a piece to check if the inside is done.

Crescent Rolls on a Stick: A Modern time favorite

Ingredients

- tube of refrigerated Crescent rolls
- Butter or margarine
- Jam, jelly, or honey

Steps

Using a thick green stick about 1 inch in diameter, wrap the dough in a crescent roll spiral fashion around the tip of the stick. Leave space with the spiral for the heat to reach all of the dough. Press the ends of the dough to the stick to stick to the stick..... Hold the stick over coals for 15-20 min., frequently turning as you salivate. When golden brown, slip the roll of the stick and spread with butter, jam, jelly, or honey. plan for 1-3 rolls per serving.

Camp Crackers

They taste great and are easy to make. Just add water and cook them anywhere you may roam. (This recipe starts by using the Bannock mix with a slight adjustment in process and the water element.) This single serving recipe will make 6-8 "round style" crackers

Ingredients

- 1 cup flour
- 1/3 c. water
- baking powder
- dash salt

Steps

Mix bannock ingredients by adding the water to the flour in a small container like a camp cup. Mix well and roll to make a small "dough ball." Cut/divide the dough into 6 equal parts and roll them into small dough balls. Heat a pan to medium/high heat temp. (A thin coat of oil, lard or butter, or even dry flour at this point on the pan's cooking surface will help keep the dough from sticking. Ensure the dough ball is floured on the outside and not sticky. This is the real trick when making a crispy cracker that won't stick to the surface of the cooking vessel.

The small dough balls are flattened into 2-3" disks about 1/4" thick or less. Place them in the pan, and using a fork, push through the center of the cracker to create a bunch of tiny holes. This helps cook the crackers evenly and helps to crisp them up! After about 1 minute, flip one to test. It should be slightly golden brown on one side. When it's done to your liking, flip and repeat. Remove crackers and eat hot or let cool and enjoy later or on the trail.

Apple Pudding

Wrapping dough around the apple

If you are expecting Jell-O-style pudding, this isn't it. Colonial

America was still attached to many English recipes during the 17th century or Longhunter era. English pudding consisted of more solid meat or fruit varieties and was typically nowhere near as sweet as to-day's food. This pudding is one recipe that explorers carried out along the frontier that I have adapted for the modern camper.

Ingredients

- 1 Small Apple
- 1 Small Candy Bar
- 1 T Sugar
- 1 tsp. Cinnamon
- 2 c. flour
- 2 Qt Pot
- Water
- Bandanna or thin rag

Steps

Begin by making a firm dough ball with flour and water. Add a heavy pinch of cinnamon and sugar to the flour before mixing. You want enough flour to wrap around your apple, so adjust accordingly. Roll out your dough to where it looks like it will wrap around your apple. Core the apple by cutting the center from the top down. Inserting a candy bar into the center, we like the fun-size Snickers bars. Next, wrap the apple in your dough ball, mix up your remaining cinnamon and sugar, and roll your dough ball around in the mixture.

Take a bandanna or thin rag and wrap it around the dough ball like it's inside a bag. It should be snug and not loose around the dough. The fabric will keep everything together while cooking. Drop the ragged dough into a cooking pot and boil it for 45-60 minutes. Allow cooling before cutting to serve. You'll have what is similar to fried apples with melted chocolate and a wet pastry full of carbohydrates and energy that multi-day campers enjoy.

Fresh Apple Pudding, a great camp treat

40

Paw-Paw Bread

Freshly harvested paw-paw

Paw-Paws are a native fruit found in the Eastern woodlands that can grow virtually anywhere in the continental United States. Upon moving to our land, my dad and I spent months combing over its resources identifying trees and plants, but never found paw-paw. I ran dozens of classes a year and had students identifying and cleaning dead debris along the way, but it wasn't until several years later that we stumbled into our paw-paw grove. During a challenging class, battling extremes of heat and rain, we sat under the oasis of fruit in the late

123

summer, just in time for harvest. While paw-paw can be eaten raw, it's delicious when used in bread-making recipes and serves as a wonderful sweet treat. It's often described as a banana-like custard; it can, of course, be more tart or sweet depending on when you harvest the fruit-and the harvest window is brief, lasting only 30-days on average.

Ingredients

- 1 c. melted butter
- 2 c. sugar
- 4 eggs
- 2 c. Paw Paw pulp
- 1 T lemon juice
- 4 c. Sifted all-purpose flour
- 2 tsp baking powder
- 3 c. chopped pecans

Steps

Preheat the oven to 375 F. In a large mixing bowl, beat butter, sugar, and eggs. Add Paw Paw pulp and lemon juice and beat together. Grease two 9x4x2-inch loaf pans, or line a #12 Dutch oven with waxed paper after greasing the cast iron. Sift the flour and baking powder together and stir into the batter. Stir in the pecan pieces and scrape the batter into the loaf pans or Dutch oven—bake for 1 hour and 15 minutes. The top corners of the loaves will become crisp.

41

Garlic Mustard Potatoes

This recipe is one Greg, an instructor at our school has shared with his family for many years. It also works as a potato salad once the potatoes are thinly sliced. Equally delicious warm over a campfire, the wood stove, or in your kitchen as a weekday side dish, it's easily tailored to your tastes and various ingredients you have on hand.

Ingredients

- 2 lbs mini potatoes (we use several different varieties from our garden)
- 4 TBsp Olive Oil
- 3 TBsp shallots finely chopped or grated
- 3 tsp Dijon mustard (we use anything we have except American yellow mustard)
- 1 tsp red wine vinegar
- 1/3 cup fresh chopped herbs. Any combination of garlic mustard, wild onion, wood sorrel, oregano, thyme, parsley, tarragon, etc.
- Salt and pepper to taste

Steps

Boil potatoes in salted water until tender, approx 6-8 minutes, Heat oil in a skillet over medium heat. Add onion and garlic until translucent. Remove from heat and whisk in mustard, vinegar, and herbs. Drain potatoes and put them into a serving dish. Pour warm dressing* over potatoes and toss until evenly coated. Salt and pepper to taste.

*This dressing is amazing brushed over grilled fish!

42

No Dough Pizza

There are times when you simply crave pizza. Pizza quickly becomes a topic of discussion when we've been running classes for a week or longer. Being tired from hiking and teaching, I rarely wanted to make pizza dough or carry something requiring refrigeration with me. A couple of blocks of cheese and a log of pepperoni could always be found in almost every camp I've been involved in over the past twenty years.

We often use sausage in camps, and I would often precook mine to get a couple of meals out of it afterward. Well, my friend, this is all we need to make an amazing, keto-friendly pizza. This pizza can be cooked on the bottom of a Bushpot, the lid of a cast iron pot, or on a sheet of metal just as well as a baking sheet.

Ingredients

- Large Handful of grated/shredded Cheddar Cheese
- A handful of Mozzarella Cheese
- Pepperoni Slices
- Small handful of cooked sausage, jerky, or bacon
- Optional: Tomato slices or 1 T pizza sauce

Steps

If available, take a slice of pepperoni or other oil, and grease your cooking service. Evenly spread a large handful of cheddar cheese on the cooking surface and melt until the edges turn a light brown. Allow cooling for 2-3 minutes. Add sauce if available or desired, then layer mozzarella, pepperoni, sausage, and another pinch of mozzarella. Place back onto the heat and cook until edges turn brown and contents are warm. Remove from heat and allow to cool for up to 5 minutes. You roll up the blend from the cooking surface and enjoy it as a rolled pizza.

43

Buffalo Chicken Taco

Buffalo-style Chicken is usually made into a dip and served at Super
Bowl parties. My daughter has made it one of her weekly staple meals,
and we now use it in various ways. One of my favorite ways to eat it
is in taco form. This method is easy at camp and makes a fast snack

or keto-friendly meal. You can also spoon this chicken mixture into avocados or tortilla wraps for amazing campfire burritos.

Ingredients

1 block of cream cheese
1 can of pulled chicken
1/4 stick of butter
2 T Frank's Red Hot Sauce (adjust to taste)
1 c. cheddar cheese

Steps

Melt butter in a heated cook pot, add a can of chicken, and brown it. Add a block of cream cheese, then cook until melted; mix ingredients well. Add red hot sauce and mix well. Adjust the exact amount to taste (mild or hot). Remove mixture from heat, and on a flat cooking surface, spread out two 1/2 c. piles of cheddar cheese, cook on waxed paper if available. Melt the cheese and cook until edges are golden brown, then remove from heat and allow to cool. Spoon the buffalo chicken mix onto the cheese to make tacos.

44

Light-weight Bag Meals

When you're hiking or need to travel light, some zip-lock bags, rice, eggs, and simple ingredients can create a variety of high-energy meals to fuel you along the trail.

Scrambled Egg Variations

Mix with a fork: or mix in ZIP lock Bag, zip tight and mash with fingers or shake it up

- 8 T powdered eggs
- 4 T water
- Salt/pepper to taste

Good add-ons:

- 4 T Shredded Cheddar, Jack, or Swiss cheese
- 4 T powdered cheese
- 3 T dry onions or peppers
- 4 T Dry mushroom pieces
- 1 T Bacon bar (Wilson's) or BACOS

- 3 T Rinsed shredded dried beef
- 1 T dried crushed tomato slices
- Dash Chili powder

Quick Rice Minute Rice Bag

- 1/2 c Minute rice
- 1/2 c water

Place 1/2 cup Minute rice in a heavy freezer zip lock bag, add 1/2 cup boiling water to the bag, and wait 3 minutes. Makes 1 serving, 3/4 cup cooked. Add butter pads and salt. Multiply the recipe by the number to serve. No pot, No mess. Add a package of Cup-of- Creamed Soup or foraged herbs and have the better part of a meal.

Energy Bag

- 1/4 c Oats
- 1/4 c peanut butter
- 1/4 c raisins or cranberries

Mix the ingredients in a bag with your fingers and roll inside the bag until a ball or bar is formed. Eat like an energy bar.

45

Maple Bacon Biscuits

This treat can be cooked in a reflector oven or a Dutch oven. The sweet and salty flavor combination is a welcome treat in cold weather camps where warm biscuits fill the soul.

Ingredients

- 1 can of Flaky biscuits

- 1/2 lb chopped bacon
- 1 c brown sugar
- Honey

Steps

Lay biscuits onto the cooking surface and cover with brown sugar and bacon. Cook the biscuits until golden brown. Once removed from heat, drizzle with honey while still warm.

Author

Dr. Jason Hunt is the Founder and CEO of Campcraft Outdoors, a softgoods manufacturing and preparedness training company located in Kentucky. His survival and outdoor knowledge are backed by thousands of man-hours in the field, where he trained many of today's top bushcraft instructors. Jason frequently contributes to Backwoods Survival Guide and Prepper's Survival Guide Magazines. His degrees are in church ministry, practical theology, and outdoor ministry leadership. Jason is also a wilderness emergency medicine instructor and volunteer firefighter with multiple specialty rescue qualifications. He's the author of *The Gospel of Survival* and co-author of *Bushcraft First Aid* with Dave Canterbury.

Contributors

Jamie L. Burleigh is an Outdoor Skills Instructor and CoFounder of the Old World Alliance. He's been actively teaching at select outdoor schools and reservations since 1992. Jamie frequently contributes to trade magazines and periodicals and has authored a series of books for Creek Stewart's Pocket Field Guide series. He was the Host of the Television program Outdoor Explorer which aired in Michigan and has worked with National Geographic. He has spent thousands of hours afield teaching people from all walks of life how to pursue the outdoor lifestyle. Jamie is an acclaimed camp cook and enjoys sharing the cooking skills and recipes of the North woods and Native culture.

Greg Laughlin came to Campcraft in 2016, earning his instructor certification in 2018. He currently teaches firearms and medical-related classes. He grew up in Western New York with a large Polish and Italian family. As a child, Sundays usually involved huge meals of Polish and Italian dishes with dozens of relatives, often staying until well after dark, eating and telling stories. His career in law enforcement has taken him to nearly three dozen foreign countries, using shared meals and the universal love of good food to network and break down social, language, and cultural barriers. He has amassed a collection of cookbooks, many documenting his travels to South/Central America and Europe. He enjoys hunting, gardening, and using harvested items to create various internationally inspired dishes.

Resources

Come visit our website at www.CampcraftOutdoors.com, where you will find a variety of outdoor gear, tools, and information to make your adventures more fun and safer. As a special thanks for purchasing this book, please use the code "CAMPCOOK" at checkout to save 15% off your next purchase*.

*Code is good for one use per customer.